SALMACIS

BECOMING NOT QUITE A WOMAN

salmacis

becoming not quite a woman

ELIZABETH TRAIN-BROWN

RENARD PRESS

RENARD PRESS LTD

124 City Road
London EC1V 2NX
United Kingdom
info@renardpress.com
020 8050 2928

www.renardpress.com

salmacis: becoming not quite a woman first published by Renard Press Ltd in 2022

Text © Elizabeth Train-Brown, 2022

Cover design by Will Dady

Printed in the United Kingdom by Severn

ISBN: 978-1-913724-89-4

9 8 7 6 5 4 3 2

Renard Press is proud to be a climate positive publisher, removing more carbon from the air than we emit and planting a small forest. For more information see renardpress.com/eco.

CONTENTS

Salmacis

the serpent had nothing to do with it 9

as told in hair 11

gods, monsters and complex ptsd 15

blood of the covenant / waters of the womb 17

you pray your way and i'll pray mine 19

ovid tells it best 21

the queen of hearts 23

orlando / orlanda 25

3 a.m. voice notes on snapchat 27

tesco trolleys, sambuca and old photos 29

lessons i almost learned 31

chasing my therapist to a rave in the woods 33

the bearers of lightning still weather the storm 35

we are just bats 37

a man once called me babel instead of baby 39

what blood won't tell you 43

we all watch the same gods 45

have you ever faked your own death and run away
  with a ferrier? 47

fire for a throne and despair for a god 51

writing is easy as breathing 53

i call her a different name in front of her parents 55

it's not just demons who make deals at crossroads 57

a boy in a nightclub alley once called me a siren 59

daphne 61

shh 63

acknowledgements 65

SALMACIS

BECOMING NOT QUITE A WOMAN

The key to success is to question your gender three times before breakfast and throw yourself at water nymphs.

the serpent had nothing to do with it

i bit deep
into the forbidden fruit
clutched it to the hollow of my chest
folded myself into the floor
and

        howled

screamed my lungs raw and burning
shattered my teeth
tore apart eden
trying to fill this ache behind my womb
that tasted divinity
and was still broken

as told in hair

i was born in a tangle
of blood and cord and hair
screaming

i knotted myself
in my mother's purple-dyed mane
clutched the strands behind her ears

and i was reborn in hair
when it clumped with blood
sticky
between legs that had never been hairy
till now

i lived
breathing the air through a fringe
down to my chin, air
like the dust from moths' wings
like the sooty cross on the brow
of children

then
i shaved my head

you can't part the tide
of someone's hair
if it's not there

can't run it through your fingers
can't pull me heavenwards

men might lick their thumbs
and wipe away my name
but i'll rewrite it

i grew
i hid dye in the showers
painted my hair in the sink
left strands of blue between pages
of books

i told children what vegetables
turn hair orange pink green
i'll tell you too
i'll help you plait your hair
with glitter and pine cones
if you ask

but mostly
i'll show you how to wrap it
around yourself
and disappear

so that when i'm old
my hair will grow silver
so thick and untamed
that after my mother dies
no one will ever see my eyes again

gods, monsters and
complex ptsd

i feel unravelled
i feel like scripture
i feel like the words of prophets
torn apart
       translated
            retranslated
rewritten
       spread to countries that don't care
what i have to say.

i feel like taking out the middle man
taking out the writer
the pen
the page
burrowing my face through the undergrowth
slithering through the cracks
of a confession booth
and whispering my sins
through a mouthful of leaves.

i feel like when someone drops a book
in a bath
i feel like the terms and conditions

i feel like a woman's words
                    in a man's book.
there
        but in his voice.

blood of the covenant / waters of the womb

i am drinking sauvignon

               while my housemate shags upstairs
and i will write poetry
before the night is through.

there is pinot noir

               on an unfinished essay
and reheated pasta
that's already gone cold.

i am bleeding merlot

               between my legs
and some point this week
i must wash the blood from my sheets

and hang them over our banister
to dry.

you pray your way and
i'll pray mine

there are times i could almost forgive my body
　　　　for having breasts
could unwind these bandages i know i shouldn't use
　　　　and swim naked

have you ever seen the swans in public fountains?

but while i stand in the shower
　　　　and face away from the mirror
　　　　watching honey-red suds
　　　　　　　disappear
　　　　down plugholes and pipes and into the sea
all i can think is that aphrodite
　　　　was born from the severed penis of a god
　　　　– so what would come of my tits?

ovid tells it best

i sit in a bath
with pink bubbles
cupping bits of my body
that i don't recognise

this is my lake salmacis
and i am the wild nymph
with a hollow in her belly
and nothing between her legs

the queen of hearts

she kisses strangers
won't learn new names
doesn't care where you're from
or why a raven
is like a writing desk

cuts herself
to watch the blood flow
backward
slug into that yawning ache
where she rests her crown

uneasy lies the head

she'll let anyone
between her legs
has tasted everyone
in wonderland
and they're all out
before the moon is up
because the queen sleeps alone

sleeps with purpled fingers
a dagger in either hand
and she never bares her chest
no one knows
the double-time staccato
between her ribs
the calcified grit
the bleeding cave
where she ripped apart
the lace of her throat
crying out the name
no one will call her

orlando / orlanda

she is the thing rattling dry grass together,
shaking them like bars on a cage,
like thigh bones looped for a skirt.
her mouth is stained with the juice from red fruits
with the fruit she plucked from my womb,
the song of the serpent still ringing in her ears,
and she will throw apart concrete to find me,
will raze these buildings to the ground
with a smile on her face and the smell of my sweat
teasing her tongue
                    vici vici
you can feel my pulse through the scars on my chest.

3 a.m. voice notes
on snapchat

i have never coaxed poetry from my heart.
more – it occurs inside me unforgivingly and without
warning, rushing from the banks of my veins,
spilling from my synapses before it can spill through ink.
these sudden metaphors and images conjured from smoke
while my mind locks the car doors and tries to cook itself
alive are what keep me writing, keep me devouring
myself, tearing the skin from my back, unlacing
my spine for you to wrap like fox or mink around your neck,
the shiver of my nightmares dripping from your ears
like pearls. these rolling seizures race up my shoulders,
spiders in enamel and lace, crawling things in my flesh
so deep the doctor thinks twice before saying cancer
or pregnancy – and you may read this and wonder
at the lyrics, the lines, the way you can almost hear
my words in your voice as i write about knotting
my bedsheets together and staring between the window
and the chandelier, but it was only chance that put a pen
in my hand before a knife.

tesco trolleys, sambuca
and old photos

I

on the wind i can hear someone else's hum
the rumble of music in someone else's throat
like writing poetry on someone else's keyboard
like brushing an eyelash from the cheek
of someone else's child

II

one night, we walked from the club to the train station
i tossed pennies on to the tracks
you climbed up the bridge to scream someone's name
i lost you when i disappeared on board a rickety
two-carriage mule
and neither i nor you nor the train
knew where we would wake up the next morning
knew which stop i'd get off at
listening to the announcer like choosing a winning horse
waiting for the hairs on my arm to stand up
for the moon to spin the other way

III

i've never won a bet
but i saw god in the bathroom mirror
and found my mother's maiden name
carved beneath a seat

lessons i almost learned

sambuca doesn't taste half as good
when you didn't buy it with rent money
                        ask anyone
and you've never felt your ankles
snap so *deliciously*
than when you roll them over
in a pair of heels so high
you could spit on a man's head

sometimes,
just don't eat. don't shower. don't check
the letters on pills you find in the carpet
before you swallow them
down a neck of straight vodka straight from
the bottle, tongue the glass of what you
will be going home with tonight

oh, and
laundry is overrated and ironing is a con
take me, for instance:

i'm on my last
pair of knickers, the ones i bought 2 sizes up
that hang from my ass like the lacy skin
of another woman. i think of how many of us
we could fit in these. think about
how many times i pulled these on as a girl,
held clumps of belly between my fingers
and thought about cutting it off

i don't think i've ever felt so cold
than when i saw my dad cry
or when i tumbled into a gutter
folded
      like a
          paper swan
and slept in the rain.

the older you get,
the less chocolate easter brings
but what they don't tell you
is you can buy a bag of creme eggs
for a quid at the festival market in morecambe
and maybe 1 in 10 people get type 2 diabetes
but that means 9 in 10 don't.

chasing my therapist
to a rave
in the woods

it's all very good telling me to breathe in for 4

           hold for 4

           breathe out for 4

           hold for 4

and that's great that's super

that's 18 months of my life i waited to see a doctor

to be told   breathe in for 4

           hold for 4

           breathe out for 4

           hold for 4

breathe myself in for 4 hear nothing but tide in my ears

hold myself for 4 in raging ocean the taste of day-old
    dog ends

breathe myself out for 4 roll in the waves like a car on
    tracks

hold myself for 4 5 6 7 8 drown waiting

for you to tell me to breathe back in

or i can weave my way between hot bodies
eels through nets
press forward, closer
with each seething breath of tide
slither through a crowd
find myself in the middle of a mosh pit
a thousand hungry corpses
alive and half-lidded under these lights

i can feel blood in my nose in my eyes
taste it finally on my tongue
and i chase it, coat my teeth in molly
eat through the ceiling stir the clouds
in my throat

in this raging, poisoned sea at night,

      it is just me
      and death

the bearers of lightning still
weather the storm

we never screamed at the sky together
never ran away from this place to wherever the next train
was going

you never tucked my hair behind my ear
and i never hit the ground until my knuckles broke

but i know that somewhere between here and the a15
there is a little stone church next to the road

and in it is a dent in a pew the shape of your ribs
because you told me that god could never be a woman

and i told her to strike

we are just bats

born on the wind
shorn by the sun
into these crackling
cackling flurries
                    and aren't you furious?

do you not feel that rage
that might've felt like summer
had it not boiled
in your belly
like tar
                    do you not miss it?

the sun
the sky
hell, the clouds?

do you not fly at night
and wonder
                    what sort of world
                    it is
                    in daylight?

a man once called me babel
instead of baby

i suppose after all this
i will be just as predictable as you thought me
i will slit the tight skin knotted over my spine
unfurl my ribs into two great wings
and clatter my way up to heaven.

i will drag floating saints down by the scruff of their neck
send them hurtling back to earth
trailing their ice tails   scrabbling for their halos
for whatever kept them holy.

i will claw my way over a ledge of cloud
look god in the eye   spit at his feet
maybe cry.

i think he will still love me.

he will smell morning-cured whiskey
see the sleep crusting my eyes   day-old mascara.

when he pulls me through the gates
he will feel the sheen of sweat
like a layer of soot on a burn victim
that burrows into pores and still turns fingers black
five, ten, a hundred years later.

he will feel these bones beneath the silk of my flesh
feel how they're crooked and carved and
some of them hollow, marked by twin holes,
the shape of your eye teeth.

he will lazily finger-knit my spine back together
with all the dawdling devotion one affords
to tracing the letters of a stranger's tombstone
in hands as small as unborn cells
      as big as whatever eats stars.

he will kiss that spot between my shoulders
and i will flinch
and he will know why
and we will not hold hands through the gates of heaven,
not before a thousand turns of the sun
has withered away and replaced this skin you touched
                                  bruised
not before i have peeled away the pages
of my arms, my legs, my back,
my face
knotted together my veins, my lungs, my hair, my shadow
cast this bundle of tired matter from thunderclouds
watched it twist in the air, resettle,
perch in the dark yawning space
behind a stranger's navel.

not before i have prayed in the rain,
washed the blood from these old bones,
not before i have stripped away everything
that remembers you and stepped into heaven
as a naked star.

i take his hand. my pulse does not jump.

what blood won't tell you

                i have a habit
        of peeling away my skin
        carding my fingers through hot arteries
        and painting the roses red.
        i close my eyes and let my fingers
        glide through heart-shadow
        glide across stolen office paper
        glide into lyrics that always
        seem to make sense
        when i read them back
        but still don't quite convey that
                1) i am not quite a woman
        and 2) i don't keep knives in the house
                when i am alone.

we all watch the same gods

i sit on a second-hand mattress that i never covered
because it still smells like another woman
like another time
and i think about why god made night first.

there is grime on this window
and a spreading crack i never fixed
that slices the pads of my fingers.
i trace the moon as she moves across the sky,
streak red into black,
know that she is the oldest god
with the deepest laugh
that she circles this quiet earth
so, when the world whirs and resettles itself,
without letting us breathe,
she hangs in the sky, the too-changing sky,
like a coin found suddenly in the pocket
when our hands don't know where else to be,
or some small thing like a silver cross on the end of a chain
to smooth, mindlessly, between the fingers
or hold on the tongue, between the lips, like prayer.

i watch the moon ripen
the smatter of stars, the drip-drip of white blood,
imagine falling off this earth into that gusset runner.

this house is old, moans and creaks in the sun,
but even this house is quiet at night.
i smooth the moon between my fingers.

have you ever faked
your own death and run away
with a ferrier?

i saw her again today.
a pair of moth-white eyes lurking
in the night,
toes poking under the curtains.

some lost and forgotten soul,
a woman in white,
whispering her name like a hymn
                    like sin.

in the bathroom mirror,
i glide my finger through steam, write,

who are you

stand naked, dripping,
read as the words appear –

47

SALMACIS

the ferrier of the styx
run

i feel her drift in my shadow
like a stowaway.
i burn food, play loud music,
turn the telly up, put the phone on speaker.

sometimes she sits
at the end of my bed,
her dark weight on my feet;
my dark weight in her hand.
i imagine her soaking in the warmth
of my sheets –
can we really feel sunlight through glass?

in bed, i read aloud,
speak aloud, pray,
muse about my day,

dream i feel breath on the air.

in window reflections, i see her
and picture those eyes:
livid and flashing like they do in the dark.
picture those lips:
flush and warm and plump
with not-quite-life.

i drink alone, at home,
and card my fingers through the air,

stroke her hair,
whisper cheap nothings that sigh
through the emptiness
like smoke
and disappear.

i hold my head under bathwater
a beat too long
and taste her breath
on my tongue.

fire for a throne
and despair for a god

the devil did not look at me
      like i thought he would.
did not speak
      like i thought he would.

it was not so much in his voice
      as it was in his lips –
they moved like continents
         rising and falling together
            the way the world was once made.
  smoky
      wordless
         because the devil does not care
            about our *and*s and *that*s
               and *me*s and *you*s.

he's had too long to practice
      being heard
      over the sounds of chaos

and we feel him speak
    the way clouds feel
        mountains knife through their belly.

    talk to me
        we whisper, gasping,
    speak to me again.

writing is easy
as breathing

easy as waking up stitches in my throat
the phantom of your fingers around my neck

easy as choking on your words in my mouth
screaming howling into the wind
shattering snow flaying the world alive
with the way your old breath sings out
between my   lips

easy as cradling the weight of smoke
in the dip of my tongue
a sinner cradling tired rosaries
between   calluses

easy as dancing in the middle
of a   housefire
gulping down this old life into these old lungs
why rush in to save the photo albums
when you can swallow them black
                         vomit them black

i gasp out the wreckage of my past
to you
a baby bird showing you what they've learned
          that they're full

i call her
a different name
in front of her parents

it's strange sharing a bed with her
we both know
that she is not gilled
like i am
that she strains for each breath
in this underwater world.
she won't bear her chest
though she knows i know
she is not scaled there
like i am
and she will never remove
her long skirts
her crab nets of silk
that make her feel both human
and not human.
but she doesn't mind it
when i slide the shawl from her shoulders

trace her land-made skin
with my sea lips
and tell her
people don't need fins
to swim in the sea.

it's not just demons
who make deals
at crossroads

you have her eyes
               hekate's
          like white wine
          like chaos.

you probably have her mouth
                         too
but i can't concentrate
long enough
when you start giggling
against my collarbone –

all i can think of
is how your breath feels
                      skating
over my chest
as you tell me

57

how sirens spring
from the women
who throw themselves
                off cliffs

how vampires are the women
who drink blood
between the legs of
                lovers

how selkies cast off
their woman-skins
fall into the sea
                and vanish.

a boy in a nightclub alley once
called me a siren

i am clutching the underbelly of a shark
it's a greenland shark, the kind that swims through icy seas
the kind that lives for hundreds of years
the kind that lives blindly in the dark
its sight harvested by two parasitic worms dangling from its eyes
until they all die together.

does it know what it looks like?
does it know what these seas are, what this sensation is on its skin?
what if two greenland sharks passed each other?
not close but perhaps just far enough away
that i could see the other shark
but they'd never know they were within
touching distance
of each other.

i am clutching the underbelly of a shark.
it won't bite me
i won't be a shark-horror-flick victim in a red bikini

whose face the director forgets later.
i'm wearing a wedding dress, actually.
and it's my mother's, if you must know.
and this shark
that does not know me
that will never see my face
but will feel the shape of it pressed against its belly
will let me wrap my arms around what of it i can,
hold it
and ask for no more.

daphne

and after the men call me moses
for claving this church ash tree in two,
i will crawl inside the hole i made
and die there

i will shrink away until i am half my size
until i am an afterthought
until i slip right through the earth
disappear between crumbs of soil
and offer what is left of me
to the earthworms, to the woodlice
grow white roots from the stumps of my limbs
poke out of these upside-down heavens
stroke sunlight like stroking a stray cat
because – after all – sunlight
ought to make a noise
and why shouldn't it purr?

if they found my body
folded over like a paper swan in a storm drain
they would try to piece together

my bones my hair my hands
call me jane doe, smooth out my skin
lay out this sliver of parchment
where the world can read me
call me a tragedy, slather me
in formaldehyde, bury me
under concrete, one man's height
below where the sun,
that ginger tom,
can butt its head against my leg

when you tangle in my leaves
tumble into the hollow neck of my tree
and fall into my body's arms.
don't scream

don't point them to this coffin,

child,
whisper another name for the sun
for a god
and let me rest

the rumbling purr of a star
in my chest

shh

she put her finger to my lips
said
this –
this dip here
this is from where they tell you to keep quiet
the split second before you fall to earth
flop out of a scarlet canal
scream yourself into the world

this is where that being
that Being
kisses
presses their finger
says
'forget me'

acknowledgements

Thank you to my parents, my family (blood and water alike), William Farr LGBTQ+ Space and the Birchall Trust, without whom neither I nor this pamphlet would be here.

'as told in hair' was first published in *The Heart of Pride* by Quillkeeper's Press as 'hair'.

'gods, monsters and complex ptsd' was first published in *Rattle* as Artist's Choice in the 2021 Ekphrastic Challenge.

'blood of the covenant / waters of the womb' was first published in *en bloc* as 'merlot'.

'you pray your way and i'll pray mine' was first published in *14 Poems* as 'notes from (just over) the edge'.

'ovid tells it best' was first published in *The Heart of Pride* by Quillkeeper's Press.

'orlando / orlanda' was first published in *Poet of the Year 2021 Anthology* by *Canterbury Festival*, as 'orlando/salmacis'.

'the bearers of lightning still weather the storm' was first published in *A Room of One's Own*.

'we are just bats' was first published in *Abridged*.

'we all watch the same gods' was first published in *The Cannon's Mouth* as 'We watch the same gods'.

'have you ever faked your own death and run away with a ferrier?' was first published in the *2021 Young Poets Prize* under 'Best Submissions' by *Stratford Literary Festival* as 'Standing in the boat'.

'it's not just demons who make deals at crossroads' was first published in *The Writing Disorder* as 'I buried my heart at a crossroad'.

'shh' was first published in *Blue Marble Review*.

about the poet

ELIZABETH TRAIN-BROWN is a poet and writer whose work has been published internationally in various anthologies and journals. Their journalism on discrimination, asexuality, transgender issues and polyamory has also received widespread recognition. Outside of writing, Elizabeth follows in her parents' footsteps as a circus performer and fortune teller. *Salmacis* is their first collection.

BETHTRAINBROWN.JOURNOPORTFOLIO.COM